C000294439

LITTLE SPROUTS MONTESSORI
THE STUDIO
72 SOMANI ROAD
QUAXATANE J.H. 30313/6

THE
SQUIRREL
IN TOWN

STANLEY COOK

THE SQUIRREL IN TOWN

and other nature poems

Illustrated by Liz Graham-Yooll

Blackie

Acknowledgements are due to the BBC on whose Poetry Corner programme many of these poems have been broadcast.

Copyright © 1988 Stanley Cook
Illustrations © 1988 Liz Graham-Yooll
First published 1988 by Blackie and Son Ltd

All rights reserved. No part of this publication may be reproduced, stored in a retrieval system, or transmitted in any form or by any means, electronic, mechanical, photocopying, recording or otherwise without the written permission of the Publishers.

British Library Cataloguing in Publication Data
Cook, Stanley
The squirrel in town and other nature poems.
I. Title
821'.914   PZ8.3

ISBN 0-216-92271-2

Blackie and Son Ltd
7 Leicester Place
London WC2H 7BP

Printed in Great Britain by
Thomson Litho Ltd, East Kilbride, Scotland

To Richard and Eloise

About the Author

Stanley Cook was born in Austerfield, South Yorkshire. He read English at Oxford and then taught in schools in Lancashire and Yorkshire. From 1969 to 1981 he lectured in English Studies at Huddersfield Polytechnic. He has had several collections of adult poetry published, including *Form Photograph*, *Staff Photograph*, *Alphabet* and *Selected Poems* and he won first prize in the Cheltenham Festival Poetry Competition in 1972. *The Squirrel in Town* is Stanley Cook's first collection of poems for children and was written expressly for children in infant schools. He began work on the poems while his wife was teaching at Ellesmere Road First School in Sheffield and now regularly visits schools to work with children on poetry.

Introduction

The squirrel referred to in the title poem of this collection was to be seen in the very centre of Sheffield, outside the main department store, with the City Hall just across the road. One change in recent years that has impressed me is the way in which Nature has come to town, a change implied by the title of this collection. A striking example is the way in which foxes have moved into the great cities, London and Birmingham for example. The fox was already present in children's imaginative experience through nursery rhymes and stories showing him as an archetype of cunning. Now he can be seen in city gardens. There is also the way in which birds, deprived of the hedgerows that farmers have removed to create superfields, are coming increasingly to rely on town and city gardens, well stocked with trees and shrubs. As far as flowers are concerned, urban dereliction has meant that in the middle of cities are areas that are virtually flowery fields.

This change is reinforced by the work of organizations such as Friends of the Earth and the Royal Society for the Protection of Birds, all encouraging children to understand and care for Nature, and by the establishment of city farms. It seems to me that, starting from the pets in the home and the classroom and the trees and flowers (even the flowering weeds) in the garden and playground, young children's interest in Nature can expand, via parks on the way, to the surrounding countryside which, from time to time, they will visit from home and from school. It is fortunate that children who live in towns and cities (the majority of the school population) can now share pleasure in Nature with children who live in the country.

Younger children are already provided with traditional material such as nursery rhymes. To complement this traditional material they need poems that appeal to their imagination through their immediate experiences and interests. Unchanging human feelings, in children as in adults, are continually expressed in changing terms as society and the environment change. Poems are the same fountain made up of different water.

One thing, however, I feel should always be remembered: that a poet needs to enter as wholly into a poem for this youngest audience as into a poem for any adult. Otherwise the children are being at least short-changed or at worst patronised. Their response has to be carefully observed. Because children of this age are unable to make a critical evaluation of a poem, they cannot express approval or disapproval as they would ten years later in the secondary school. Theirs is an all or none reaction — most endearing in one way, since if they like a poem they are unreservedly appreciative. A good poem for children is a good poem for life.

Stanley Cook

Barney and Fred

Fancy eating your bed
Like the guinea pigs Barney and Fred
Who nibble away
Wood shavings and hay.

I should never feel
Like making my house a meal
And gnawing the wood
To do my teeth good.

I never met anyone yet
Who eats the floor and carpet
Except, as I said,
Barney and Fred.

Bingo

Bingo the handsome
Long-haired guinea pig from Peru
Made his home
In our living room.

I built a box for him
And filled it with shavings and hay
But he was seldom in
And roamed the room most of the day.

Over the side of the box
He would take a peep
Then clear the top
In one big leap.

We used a baby brush
To smooth his long white hair
And covered his favourite corner
With a red carpet square.

He fancied straw baskets,
Schoolbooks, slippers
And fraying carpets
As you do dolly mixtures.

In non-stop hide-and-seek
He dodged us everywhere –
Under the table, between our feet
And round the sewing-machine and rocking
    chair.

Bingo was the wildest boy
But we loved to see
Him jump for joy
At being free.

Lizzie, the Footballing Kitten

Lizzie the kitten can twist and turn
And walk in line and climb,
Steering herself by her whiskers
And waving her tail from side to side.

Lizzie is learning football
On the carpet on the floor,
Dribbling a ball of wool
With tiny kicks of her paws.

I kick the ball with my finger,
She saves it with her claws
And the unwound wool shows where we played
Around the chairs and out of the door.

Ebony the Cat

Ebony curls her tail about her paws
And fills an empty space
Where an ornament is missing
From above the fireplace.

As smooth and black as her name,
She sits without moving an ear,
Her tiny machine of pleasure
Purring too softly for us to hear.

She listens to the whole of the house,
To the birds in the tree
And next door's noisy dog
Who isn't the tough he pretends to be.

In that jumble of sounds
She hears the turn of the key
Letting someone in
And setting Ebony free.

She dodges pats and strokes
And shoots out at the door;
Her tail stretched out like the tip of a rope,
She expresses along the garden wall.

Pip

Pip is a dog with four short legs
In four white socks of different lengths,
Who stands against the letter-box
Barking at the letters dropping down,
As if he were living on a farm
And they were cows he was herding home.

He rushes up the stairs
And barks at the window-cleaner
Outside upon his ladder
As if he were a robber.

He sits on guard over parcels
On the back seat of the car,
As if they were hens and he kept the fox
From raiding the poultry yard.

If he finds, in or out of the house,
Anything he's not sure about,
He stands there barking and carries on
Till I stroke him to let him know
There's nothing wrong.
He works so hard all week
That he deserves a sleep
In the best armchair.

Bonnie

When we walk each day in the wood
The things that interest me
Are the flowers in the grass
And leaves and birds on the trees.

But a clever dog has other things,
News of which she wants to know
And pulls me back upon the leash
While she fingers the ground with her nose.

She sticks her nose among the ivy
Like someone deep in a book,
Finding out which way
A mouse or a squirrel took.

She stiffens her tail with excitement
And while we stand on the path
A brown pincushion-like hedgehog
Slowly comes out of the grass.

The Budgie

The budgie has a bell to ring
And tunes from the radio to sing
A pot of water and a pot of seed
For when he wants to drink or feed
And every week a new sandsheet
To sharpen the claws of his bony feet.
He calls himself a pretty boy
But his only friend is a plastic toy.

But budgies fly in another land
Over miles of yellow sand
And peck the seeds that grow
And drink the streams that flow.
A crowd of uncaged budgies fly,
Green as grass or blue as sky.

The Gerbil

The gerbil stands up
Crouching like a kangaroo
Ready to hop;
To him the children he sees
Seem tall as trees;
His paws clutch
The teacher's hand
That stretches like a branch
Above the sand
Of the tiny desert
In his hutch.

My Rabbit

Anyone would think
My rabbit had spilt the ink.
His nose and ears are dipped in black
And black is spattered along his back.

I cover the floor
Of his hutch with straw
And while I clean it out
I let him run about.

Once in the garden his long ears prick
And like a kangaroo's his back legs kick.
No end of fun to watch.
No end of trouble to catch.

The Goldfish

The sides of the tank are slimy and green.
The fish goes round
Without a sound
Like a submarine.

The watersnails are slow and fat.
The fish goes round
Without a sound
Each snail inside a black old hat.

With bridges to swim beneath
The fish goes round
Without a sound
With spreads of ant eggs to eat.

Slippery and cold
The fish goes round
Without a sound
Wearing tights of shining gold.

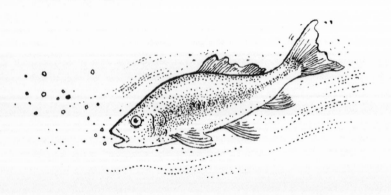

Under the Ice

After a night of frost
Ice covers the puddles
Like a pane of glass;
And the pond is frozen over
Wide as a shop window,
Where under the ice we see
The stone and water weed
And sometimes a golden gleam
From the fish that swim
In their ice-topped room.

Noah

God told Noah to build
A zoo on board a boat
And wait for the floods
To make it float.

Noah built a boat with nests,
Boxes, stables, pens,
Baskets, perches, kennels,
Hutches, hollow, holes and dens.

He cut down a forest
To make so big a boat
And the floods came round the Ark
And made it float.

It rained in the puddles
Day after day after day
Till the puddles were big as seas
And floated the Ark away.

And Noah stood on the Ark
With a parrot perched on his head
And a spider hung from his ear
By a long thin thread.

With a budgie hooked in his beard
Where Noah could hear what it said,
Mice nesting in his pocket
And a snake tied round his leg.

Noah put out the bamboo shoots
And saw that the pandas were fed.
He fetched the monkeys off the roof
And put the tigers to bed.

The Wind

The wind is a wolf
That sniffs at doors
And rattles windows
With his paws.

Hidden in the night,
He rushes round
The locked-up house,
Making angry sounds.

He leaps on the roof
And tries to drive
Away the house
And everything inside.

Tired next morning,
The wind's still there,
Snatching pieces of paper
And ruffling your hair.

He quietens down and in the end
You hardly notice him go
Whispering down the road
To find another place to blow.

Snowing

On a winter day
The flakes of snow
Fall like broken clouds
To the earth below.

As I look up
I feel the flakes
As soft as wool
Brushing my face.

The sky is a roof
That has fallen down
Scattering white pieces
Over the ground.

Rabbits and birds
That live outdoors
Fluff up their fur
And ruffle their feathers.

Though the roof has fallen
And it begins to freeze
They keep themselves warm
In their house in the fields.

Raining

Birds stop singing as the storm comes by.
Raindrops measure all the way down
From the clouds in the sky
To the puddles on the ground.

The falling balls of water
Bounce from the ground or make big bubbles
That burst against each other
As they float upon the puddles.

Leaves on the trees play ball
And bat the falling drops;
The flowers duck and hide in their petals
Until the rainstorm stops.

After the rain the sunshine comes;
The puddles make mirrors where I see
My own reflection in wellingtons
Making faces at me.

The Sun in the Sky

I watch the sun
Go high in the sky.

The sun is a big red ball.
I watch it bounce
Above the house.

No one can catch
The sun in the sky.

Night and the Stars

Night takes away
The light of day
In a black sack.

Bright white stars escape
Through holes they make
In the black sack
The night has on its back.

A Cave

A cave is a house without a door
With walls without windows and a hard stone
   floor.
A cave is a way inside the hill
Where it never rains or snows
And the wild wind never blows;
No one knows how deep it goes
To underground lakes and rivers.
A cave is a place for guarding a treasure
Of piled-up gold and silver
And when the sun is shining outside
A cave is still so dark and cold
No wonder the dragons who lived there long ago
Breathed out fire.

The Shell

In winter I put a shell to my ear
And through its telephone I hear
The sound of the sea
Speak to me.

'Are the donkeys and funfair
Boats and gulls still there?'
I say.

'The pier wading out from the land
And starfish like badges on the sand
As on my holiday?'

The whispering tide
In the shell replies,
'They will all be here
When you come next year.'

The Beach is a Sandtray

The beach is one big sandtray
Where I and the sea
That is so much bigger than me
Both want to play.

The sea brings sticks ashore
Like a dog having fun
And touches everyone
With a big wet paw.

It wants you to look
At the singing shells
And coloured pebbles
It washes up.

But I am busy scooping the sand
And letting the beach trickle
Little by little between my fingers
And out of my hand.

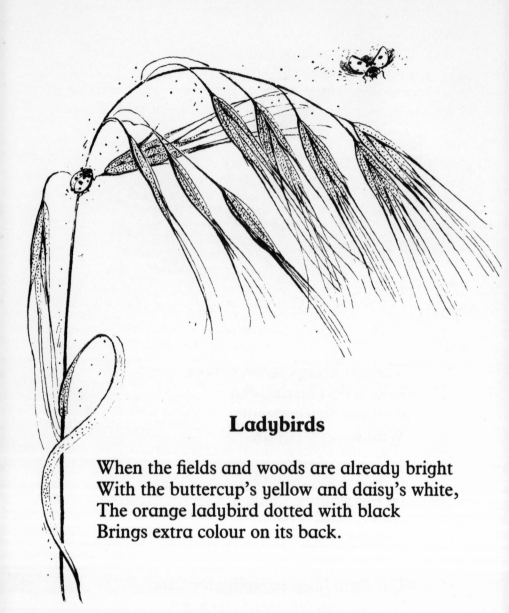

Ladybirds

When the fields and woods are already bright
With the buttercup's yellow and daisy's white,
The orange ladybird dotted with black
Brings extra colour on its back.

It climbs up ladders of grass and flies to leaves
Hanging down low on bushes and trees;
It even makes beautiful
The hairy, rough, stinging nettle.

Ladybirds can often be seen
Colouring leaves that are only plain green
And, spreading their thin wings, they sometimes
    land
Upon my sleeve or decorate my hand.

The Butterfly

The sun is on fire
In the sky
And in its warmth
Flowers open
In the garden
And the butterfly
Flutters by.

Wings widespread,
It stops to feed
At the flower-bed
And on its favourite flower
The butterfly settles
Like two extra petals.

Silverfish, Spiders and Flies

Small creatures see
That none of the space
In our classroom
Goes to waste.

Silverfish keep warm
In cracks too small
Even for children's fingers
In the floor and against the wall.

And knitting their webs
The spiders fit
Onto ledges too narrow
For children to sit.

Flies stand on the ceiling
Or circle through the air
And even in P.E.
I never climbed up there.

Creatures that look
Like pips and seeds
Sow themselves in places
No one else needs.

Tadpoles

Tadpoles are fat brown dots
That stand on their tails to nibble weed
Or swish them from side to side
To drive to places to feed:
A head with a tail
Waiting till the body comes,
Waiting for legs
To make it a frog
That climbs from the water onto a stone
And bounces slowly away to a life of its own.

Boot the Hedgehog

Boot the hedgehog
Comes to the door for his milk,
Walking in the saucer
And licking up any he's spilt.

He curls in a ball
And sticks out his spikes
At anyone he doesn't know
Or doesn't like.

A scratching cat
Or a savage big dog
Daren't lay a paw
On a curled-up hedgehog.

He curls himself up
As stiff and brown as a brush
And full of prickles
As a blackberry bush.

But he likes his milk
And likes me too.
When I fill his saucer
He licks my shoe.

The Squirrel

The squirrel's main road
Is up the trunk of an oak
And its branches are paths
Where he runs as fast
As I do on the ground
And never once falls down
But spreads his tail and legs
And glides to the top of the hedge.
I've one path and he's a hundred
Where he races overhead,
Fluttering the leaves
Of the oak and the beech.
He stops to look at me
Round the trunk of the tree
In a cheeky way
As much as to say
'Catch me if you can'
And I can't.

The Squirrel in Town

Was the squirrel looking for nuts
On the trees that grow in a row
In front of the biggest shop in town
At the edge of the busy road?

We stopped and stared at him
And he stared back at us,
But he didn't go inside the shop
Or wait at the stop to catch a bus.

He sat down underneath a tree
And took his time to make up his mind
Then darted between the passing cars
His long tail flying out behind.

Perhaps he knew of a nearby garden
With a big old tree that was just as good
For living and hiding in
As the trees in a wood.

Paws

My gloves are woollen paws
My Mother knitted for me
While we were watching
TV after tea.

They keep me as warm
In the winter cold
As the fur of the big white bears
Who live in the ice and snow.

37

The Spring Flower

I put the bulb in the ground
Weeks and weeks ago
Where it could hide
From winter's frost and snow.
    There it lies
    And shuts its eyes.

And when I had forgotten
That I had put it there
It reached its green leaves out
To test the warmth of the air.
    The bulb sits up in bed
    And puts its hands above its head.

Round a purple flower
Its green leaves opened wide
As if it were opening hands
To show a present inside.
    Up it stands
    And stretches out its hands.

Bluebells

This year and every year
The long-legged trees
Stand, now spring is here,
In a bright blue sea.

No one can count the bluebells
That gather together
Until they fill
The woods with waves of their colour.

Beneath new shining leaves
On the long-legged trees
Children gathering flowers
Paddle in a bluebell sea.

Daisies

By the roadside
And on the lawns of houses I pass
Daisies are as white
As spills of milk on the grass.

White, with yellow centres
And small and round,
Daisies are the buttons
On the coat of the ground.

And I can decorate my coat
With milk-white daisies tipped with red;
I stitch them into my buttonholes
By the stalk's green thread.

Dandelions

The dandelion have escaped,
Wearing golden crowns,
From the prison where grey, cold winter
Shut them up beneath the ground.

Cracking ground trodden hard down
And moving stones, the imprisoned Kings
Shake off dirt and bits of straw
And return to rule the spring.

Dandelions are proud bright flowers
That conquer the gardens and fields,
Surrounded by a guard
Of fierce jagged leaves.

Sunflowers

Sunflowers try
To reach as high
As the sky.
Their broad leaves climb
Two at a time
To the top of the stem
Above the children
And taller
Than the wall.

Down in the garden
The flowers turn
Towards the sun
And their petals burn
Yellow and warm.
In the sky
Is one big sun
And down below
Shine half-a-dozen
Little ones.

Thistles

Thistles are dragons growing wild
In the wind on the hillside,
Fierce green dragons
With prickling stalks for legs
And leaves for wings with a prickly edge.
With a flower like purple fire
They burn in fields or beside the road,
Puffing out thistledown seeds
That blow away like smoke.

In the Garden in Winter

In the garden in winter
One rose
Like a creamy ice-cream cornet
Still grows.

In the garden in winter
Two pears
That ripened all summer
Still hang there.

In the garden in winter
Three birds
Peck each other
And the bread.

In the garden in winter
Four trees
With leafless boughs
Comb the breeze.

In the garden in winter
Five cabbages grow
And wait to be eaten
In a row.

In the garden in winter
Six steps of stone
Are the only things
That don't feel cold.

In the garden in winter
Seven days of the week
Beneath the ground
The flower bulbs sleep.

The Flowers in Town

Among the busy streets
In the middle of the town
Is a flowery field
Where houses have been knocked down.

The men with cranes and bulldozers
Left the ground brown and bare
Except for the broken bricks
Scattered everywhere.

The ground was rough and bumpy
And there the old bricks lay
Like a set of building blocks
That hadn't been put away.

But the seeds of flowers
That were looking for a home
Travelled there on the wind
And made the place their own.

Ragweed that seems to be knitted
Out of yellow wool
And poppies like red crêpe paper
Have filled the hollows full.

High in the air, the willow herb
Raises its pointed towers
And daisies and butterfingers
Pattern the grass with flowers.

Where the people used to live
In the houses the men knocked down
Bees and butterflies are busy
In the flowers' new town.

Growing Grass

Grass grows anywhere,
Making the ground soft to the feet
And sowing the dust the wind puffs
Into holes and cracks with its yellow seed.

On tumbledown old houses
It climbs the roof to sit on top.
Grass instead of smoke
Gathers round the chimney pot.

So when we set its seed
In a trough of polystyrene
No wonder grass came up
As long as hair and beautifully green.

We planted flowers as well –
Daffodils and busy lizzie.
When the grass grew really long
We gave it a haircut with our scissors.

Farmers grow grass in fields
To feed their cows non-stop all week.
We grew grass in a trough
For our guinea pigs to eat.

Magpies

Two big black-and-white birds
That walk up and down
Inspecting the lawn
As if they had to know
It was properly mown
Are a pair of magpies
Looking for worms.

The pair of paper aeroplanes
That swoop and glide
Across the outdoor rooms
The trees make in the woods
Are magpies that fly
Away from harm.

The guards in a smart
Black-and-white uniform
Whose threats and pecks
Send back the cat
Scrambling down
The tree to the ground
Are the pair of magpies
Defending their nest.

Rooks

The tall trees sway
On a windy day
And the rooks are rocked
In their nests at the top.

Rooks sound proud,
Cawing long and loud,
As I should be
At holding on to the swaying tree.

Rooks are the crew of trees
With their sails of leaves
And tall wooden masts
In a sea of grass.

The Bluetit

In summer he practises
Gymnastics on the twigs of trees,
Holding as tightly and lightly
As the fluttering leaves.

Or when we take the milk in
We see where he has been
Snipping open the bottle top
To have a sip of cream.

In winter he performs for us,
A daring little acrobat
Clinging upside down
To a piece of fat.

From his perch in the pear tree
He walks the washing-line
Then flits to the fat on its string
At his breakfast time.

The Robin in December

When the leaves have fallen
And the days begin to shorten;
When the dark night draws its curtains
At tea-time on the sun;
When the summer flowers have gone
And we put our warm coats on –
The robin comes back to the garden.

All the rest of the year
We knew he was somewhere near
And we saw him from time to time
On the wall or the lawn or flying by,
But he never came before
Right up to the kitchen door.

Is he waiting to be drawn
To go on a Christmas card?
Is he bringing a touch of red
Now most of the roses are dead?
No: we guess why he comes
And put out seed for him and crumbs.

The Swan from the Park

It was dark
Beneath the bridge
In the park
Where the white swan
Floated on
The shadow's edge.

Suddenly
It rose to fly
Stretching out its neck
And aiming its beak
At the farthest cloud
In the sky.

It rose from the park below
Straight and swift as an arrow
Shot from a bow.

Sparrows

Does this town belong to us
Or to the sparrows I see
In the gardens and parks
And on every roof and tree?

Gangs of sparrows chase each other
Where I wait for the bus to stop
And fewer people perch in the bus
Than sparrows on the shelter top.

Who has the bigger parties
In the chilly winter-time –
The sparrows with crumbs in the garden
Or people at breakfast inside?

In the playground at school
Children and sparrows are everywhere,
But sparrows go where children can't –
Up on the roofs and into the air.

They don't look very smart
In their shabby grey and brown
But the cheeky sparrows behave
As if they owned the town.

Feeding the Pigeons

Whenever we go into town
The pigeons are waiting to be fed
As if they knew I was coming
With a bag with crusts of bread.

No wonder they're looking fat
For they're always ready to eat
And hungry and bold enough
To come right up to your feet.

They must be pleased with the crusts
For when they've filled themselves
With crumbs from the cracks in the pavement
They stroll about and nod their heads.

Flowering Trees

As soon as spring has come
The almond and cherry trees
Make fountains of blossom
Before they open their leaves.

The black trunk shoots straight up
And the branches break into showers
Of small but beautiful
Pink or white flowers.

When jostling breezes blow
Some of the petals fall
On the stony path below
And catch in cracks in bricks in the wall.

In playgrounds, parks and gardens
And in rows along the road
The coloured fountains come on
At the end of winter and the cold.

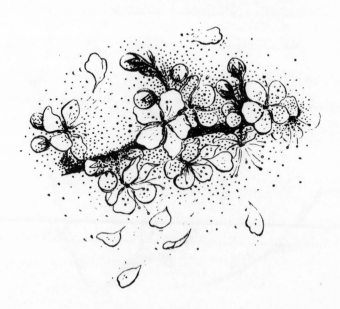

Willow Catkins

Flowers form a row
Along the twigs of willow
As soft as a kitten's nose
And grey as a kitten's toes.

The twigs rock to and fro
In the cold winds that blow
The clouds across the sky above,
But the furry gloves are warm as a glove.

The Chestnut

The chestnut kept itself
Away from me
At the top of the tree
Like a present on a shelf.

Too high for me to hit
With a stone or a stick
And with a skin too thick
For me to open it.

But when I had left it alone
The wind last night
Seized it as tight
As a dog that worries a bone.

The wind was on my side
And today I found
The chestnut on the ground
With skin split open wide.

The nut's white skin turns brown
As the skin of someone
Lying in the sun –
A present the wind has handed me down.

Falling Leaves

The leaves in autumn
Swing on the boughs
Pushed by the wind,
Backwards and forwards
Far above the ground.
The wind blows hard
And the leaves let go
Their hold,
Flying over the wood
Like a flock of birds
Flying above the house.
The wind lets them fall
Helter skelter
Towards the ground.
It sets them spinning
On a roundabout.
They land on pavements
And children watch them
And try to catch them
As they come down.
They crowd together
By walls at corners
Or play wild games.
Sometimes when you open
The kitchen door
A leaf blows in
And lies, as if it were tired
From so much playing,
On the kitchen floor.

Gathering Leaves

In autumn the falling leaves
Run races on the paths,
Tumble head over heels
And catch against the tufts of grass.

I gather them in a heap
With a stiff brush and a rake,
Though they are light as feathers
And do their best to escape.

Then I splash right into the heap
And the leaves wash over me
With a long swishing sound
Like a wave of the sea.

Christmas Trees

The Christmas trees in the forest
Stand in a long row,
Spreading their branches like arms
To catch the falling snow.

Their branches point at the moon
And the stars in the sky
And reach to catch the clouds
That go floating by.

When they come indoors
They gather in their arms
Christmas presents and tinsel
And hold bright lights and stars.

The Wood

A little wood
Of pale-faced flowers
Roofed by trees
To keep out the showers.

With a path and a stile
Instead of a door
And last year's fallen leaves
To cover the floor.

No one who went there
Ever knocked
For the house of the wood
Is always unlocked.

The Acorn that Grew

The giant oak across the road
Seemed angry one windy day,
Pelting the ground with acorns
And tossing leaves and twigs away.

One acorn landed in our garden
Wearing its shiny helmet
Of hardened light brown skin
With a spike on the end of it.

Slowly the spike grew down
Into the ground to make a root.
The side of the helmet split open
And through the gap poked a tiny shoot.

The shoot had a bud that turned to a leaf,
For packed inside an acorn
Is everything to make an oak
Shaking its angry arms at the storm.

The Oak

Its trunk is broad and strong:
The oak is the wood's strong man.

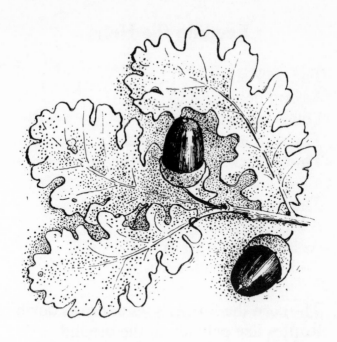

The oak grows slowly, its bark getting harder
And keeping it safe like a suit of armour.

As if for a tug-of-war, it sinks its roots
Into the ground to steady its foot.

Like a man who heaves and wrestles,
Its arms are thick with muscles;

Leaves at their fingertips sometimes stay on,
Brown and dry, all winter long.

The strong man likes a little fun –
He pelts us with acorns when autumn comes.

Feeding the Hens

The cock sings
As day begins,
Loud and proud.
The sun sets off his alarm
That wakens the rest of the farm.

The hens cluck
A kind of yawn
As he wakes them up
And fuss for their corn.

The corn the farmer's wife throws down
Rattles like pebbles on the ground
And a cheeky sparrow escapes by air
With his stolen share.

Seven Cows

Seven cows live at the end of a lane
In a shed with a field all round
Spread out like a picnic table-cloth
With walls at the edge to hold it down.

Through big brown eyes the seven cows
See stretching before their feet
Bright green food with flowers in it
That takes them most of the year to eat.

They eat plain grass once dandelions,
Daisies and buttercups are gone.
They walk across the table-cloth
And day after day their picnic goes on.

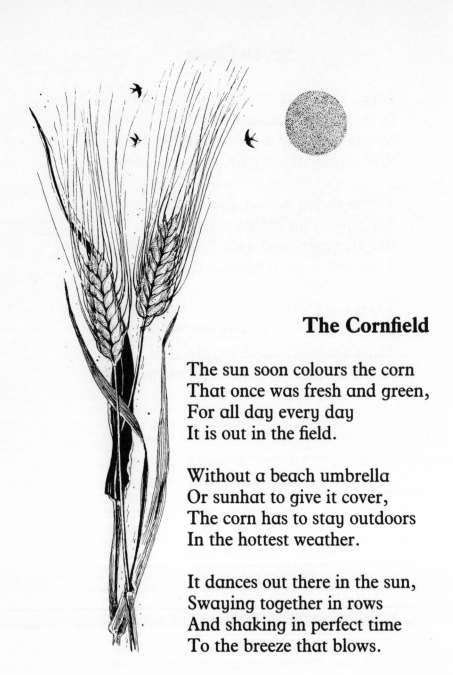

The Cornfield

The sun soon colours the corn
That once was fresh and green,
For all day every day
It is out in the field.

Without a beach umbrella
Or sunhat to give it cover,
The corn has to stay outdoors
In the hottest weather.

It dances out there in the sun,
Swaying together in rows
And shaking in perfect time
To the breeze that blows.

How Many Rows of Potatoes?

Potato plants look beautiful
Growing in farmers' fields
With white, yellow-centred flowers
And dark green leaves.

In autumn the red machine
Drives up and down
Digging out of the ground
Hundreds of pink potatoes.

How many rows of potatoes
Do I eat, fried as chips,
Roasted, mashed, boiled in their jackets
And crinkly bagfuls of crackling potato crisps?

The Apple

Hold an apple in your hand,
Pale green but streaked with red on one side
With a smooth, just sticky skin
And a sweet green smell of fields and sunshine.

A man with an apple orchard climbed
With a bag for apples hung round his neck
His ladder upstairs to the top of his tree
And this was one of the apples he picked.

It grew like this with the red-streaked side
Turned out to the sun among dark green leaves.
He held it like this as he snapped the twig –
I can nearly reach to put it back on the tree.

Apple Time

When there's warm weather
At the end of summer
The trees have their hands full
Of red-cheeked apples.

As you lie in the sun
A tree lets fall
An apple on your head
Or bounces them at your feet
Or tries to reach down
To put one in your mouth
Or drops them over the wall
For people in the street
Or rolls them over the grass
Or down the path.

When there's warm weather
At the end of summer
The trees have tricks to play
And apples to give away.

The Tree is Best at Standing Still

The tree is best at standing still
With its feet deep-rooted in the ground
As if it were someone put in the middle
Of games that children play all round.

It doesn't shelter from the rain
But holds its own umbrella of leaves
On its wooden arm over anyone
Who wants to shelter beneath.

When the wind gives the tree a push
Its branches bend and sway
And its blossom bobs about
But the wind never makes it move away.

All night it waits for the day,
All winter it waits for the spring,
Keeping places among its branches
Where any bird that wishes can perch and sing.

Index of First Lines

A cave is a house without a door 27
A little wood 63
After a night of frost 19
Among the busy streets 46
Anyone would think 16
As soon as spring has come 56
Bingo the handsome 8
Birds stop singing as the storm comes by 24
Boot the hedgehog 34
By the roadside 40
Does this town belong to us 55
Ebony curls her tail about her paws 11
Fancy eating your bed 7
Flowers form a row 58
God told Noah to build 20
Grass grows anywhere 48
Hold an apple in your hand 70
I put the bulb in the ground 38
I watch the sun 25
In autumn the falling leaves 61
In summer he practises 51
In the garden in winter 44
In winter I put a shell to my ear 28
It was dark 54
Its trunk is broad and strong 64
Lizzie the kitten can twist and turn 10
My gloves are woollen paws 37
Night takes away 26
On a winter day 23
Pip is a dog with four short legs 12
Potato plants look beautiful 69
Seven cows live at the end of the lane 67
Small creatures see 32

Sunflowers try   42
Tadpoles are fat brown dots   33
The beach is one big sandtray   28
The budgie has a bell to ring   15
The chestnut kept itself   59
The Christmas trees in the forest   62
The cock sings   66
The dandelions have escaped   41
The gerbil stands up   16
The giant oak across the road   64
The leaves in autumn   60
The sides of the tank are slimy and green   18
The squirrel's main road   35
The sun is on fire   31
The sun soon colours the corn   68
The tall trees sway   50
The tree is best at standing still   72
The wind is a wolf   22
This year and every year   39
Thistles are dragons growing wild   43
Two big black-and-white birds   49
Was the squirrel looking for nuts   36
When the fields and woods are already bright   30
When the leaves have fallen   52
When there's warm weather   71
When we walk each day in the wood   14
Whenever we go into town   56